William Wells Newell, Adelene Moffat

Words for Music

William Wells Newell, Adelene Moffat

Words for Music

ISBN/EAN: 9783337084233

Printed in Europe, USA, Canada, Australia, Japan

Cover: Foto ©Thomas Meinert / pixelio.de

More available books at **www.hansebooks.com**

WORDS FOR MUSIC

Words for Music

BY

WILLIAM WELLS NEWELL

CAMBRIDGE
CHARLES W. SEVER
𝔘𝔫𝔦𝔳𝔢𝔯𝔰𝔦𝔱𝔶 𝔅𝔬𝔬𝔨𝔰𝔱𝔬𝔯𝔢
1895

Copyright, 1895,
BY WILLIAM WELLS NEWELL.

University Press:
JOHN WILSON AND SON, CAMBRIDGE, U. S. A.

CONTENTS

	PAGE
THE FORGOTTEN HARP	9
WHEN ROSE THY STAR	11
ARISE ON MY SPIRIT LONELY	12
A WISH	13
RESERVE	14
ROSEBUD AND ROSE	15
LIEB' UND LEID	16
LOVE-THOUGHTS	17
LOVE'S MEASURE	18
CRADLE-SONG	20
THE FOUNTAIN	21
A NAY-WORD	22
THE MENDED VIOL	23
THE LAND OF THE LOST	24
BEGGARY	25
FAIRIES' HILL	27
RED-ROSE-WOOD	30
THE LAST WORDS	32
THE SISTERS	35
FUNERAL MARCH	37
THE LONELY OCEAN	39
THE FOUNT OF TEARS	40

CONTENTS

	PAGE
THE WELL OF THE WORLD'S END	42
A BIRTHDAY	43
MAY MORNING	44
THE SCARLET TANAGER	45
ORPHEUS TO APOLLO	46
THE LAKE AND THE RIVER	47
VIOLET	49
WATER-LILIES	50
MOONLIGHT	51
THE LIGHTHOUSE	52
THE STORM	53
THE FOREST	55
AN OUTLOOK	57
THOUGHT-BIRTHS	59
ANY HARPER TO HIS HARP	62
TO THE SOUL	64
DECORATION	65
GREETING	68
THE TEMPLE	69
REQUIEM	70
EROICA	71
PEACE	74
A MEMORY	75

Dear thought, I sue thee for desired relief!
Even too long thou chantest in mine ear;
I would be free another tune to hear;
Behold, I write thee on this withered leaf.

Forgive the art, that partial, hath designed
In black and white, thine act, thy glance alone,
And forfeited the soul of breathing tone;
Go seek thy life, and haply shalt thou find.

A pilgrim rove with fates and airs benign!
If fortune waft thee in a loiterer's way,
Who pondereth upon the legend, say:
"I who am no man's, fain I would be thine."

THE FORGOTTEN HARP

He found the harp, where lost it lay, the strings he
 tuned and smote;
Unloved so long, these made reply with many a
 grateful note,
To gates of life thronged eager joys impassioned to
 be born,
And sang exultingly, as chant the choristers of morn.

Within the harp, by music roused, the mind, the
 soul, awoke,
In sobbing plaint, in piercing wail, loud waves of
 passion broke;
Wild cries were hushed, the calmer dirge rolled on
 in full lament,
Then widened to a solemn flow of sorrow innocent.

Anew, by intermittent chords, returned the former strain,
In timid plea, with wistful hope, glad voices breathed again;
They rose, they swelled, a fountain pure below a bitter lake,
Mild stars above a darkened tide, a bough for Mara's sake.

The primal mirth, the sequent pain, were told by echoes dim;
The themes, concordant, met and died in movement of a hymn;
The player, ceasing, on his harp leaned silent for a while,
As shone in forward-gazing eyes a sweet and mystic smile.

WHEN ROSE THY STAR

WHEN rose thy star, thy Fate chose one of gifts that
    many be;
A golden harp the fairy made her offering to thee.

She charmed it first, the harp of gold, she sang a
    moving spell;
Delights of eld, forgotten griefs, she bade therein to
    dwell.

Strike thou the harp, the golden harp, thyself her
    music play;
In magic tones, with wild accords, repeat the fairy
    lay.

ARISE ON MY SPIRIT LONELY

ARISE on my spirit lonely, arise with thy radiance dear,
Like a star that lendeth to ocean its lustre silver and clear,
With the air of thy bosom's breathing sweet breath to the flowers give,
In thy murmur and thy silence let the soul of the music live.

Each life will be grateful, and render its present to make thee blest,
The many lamps and the lustres a jewel to bind on thy breast,
The garlands that fall in the chambers a wreath to twine in thine hair,
The feast be thy beauty's garment, and thine be the presence there.

A WISH

Go, thought, for me
Over land and sea;
Early or late,
Linger and wait.

When falls the hour,
Become a flower,
At feet to lie
Where he passeth by.

For perfume's sake,
The flower he will take,
To breathe its air,
And heedfully bear.

On he will go,
Pensive and slow:
"How came it here,
So dewy and dear?"

RESERVE

The scornful stars their boon deny
    What time Aurora glows;
The shamèd flowers turn cold and shy
    When openeth the rose.

Yet, dear, believe, no fairer face
    For me can rival thine,
And be no miser of thy grace,
    However planets shine.

I would that deeper were the night,
    And I thy star to see;
I wish me far from roses' sight,
    And thou my rose to be.

ROSEBUD AND ROSE

A FLOATING spray of your wreath,
A bud secure in its sheath,
   You strewed last night;
I saved it and thought no more;
You wished me, the dancing o'er,
   A low good-night.

I woke at the break of day;
All fragrant, beside me lay
   This rose of light.
I muse how the flower came;
Reply, if it be the same
   You strewed last night.

LIEB' UND LEID

"Sweet harp, thy mode of gladness
 To-night employ;
Awake no tone of sadness
 To darken joy."

"Dear harp, what doubts deceive thee,
 What error's thine?
Doth my rejoicing move thee
 To sob and pine?"

"Thy life, thy life to measure
 With music's chain,
I link regret to pleasure,
 And bliss to pain."

LOVE-THOUGHTS

The lake art thou, beloved,
    When the sunrise dawneth o'er;
My thoughts, they are water-lilies,
    That float and blow by the shore.

The forest art thou, beloved,
    Full leafy in warm July;
My thoughts, they are crimson roses,
    That twine and blossom by.

The heaven art thou, beloved,
    So holy at still midnight;
My thoughts, they are stars of summer,
    That beam with a peaceful light.

LOVE'S MEASURE

"Beloved, tell,
If thou lovest me well."

"I love thee with days, as many as be,
And I love thee with all that the daybeams see;
I love thee with every river that flows,
I love thee with the heart of the rose."

"Yet tell, yet tell,
If thou lovest me well."

"I love thee with nights, so holy and deep,
I love thee with all the kingdoms of sleep;
I love thee with many a glorious star,
I love thee with moons, that golden are."

"Yet tell, yet tell,
If thou lovest me well."

LOVE'S MEASURE

"I love thee with the blue eyes of a child,
I love thee with his lisping mild;
I love thee with the orient morn
On the brow of youth when the spirit is born."

  "Yet tell, yet tell,
   If thou lovest me well."

"I love thee with sorrows, I love thee with tears,
I love thee with wreck of the darkening years;
I love thee with the silence and peace
Of angel who waiteth for soul's release."

  "Cease, cease to tell,
   For thou lovest me well."

CRADLE-SONG

Mary gave to Jesus birth,
In her arms held heaven and earth,
   So clasp I thee!

Mary lulled her babe to sleep,
Slumber calm did Jesus keep,
   Hush thou for me!

Mary knelt above her child,
Jesus opened eyes and smiled,
   Smile thou on me!

Jesus held out arms so blest,
Mary caught him to her breast,
   So take I thee!

THE FOUNTAIN

She rested her jar on the fountain stone;
The water flowed, and the water shone.

"Give me to drink of thy water cold,
I'll pay thee with silver, I'll pay thee with gold."

"Thy silver and gold, they are little to me;
I pour for another, I pour for thee."

She held to his lips the pitcher agleam,
She shed on his hands a silvery stream.

"Thou hast had thy fill of the flowing well,
Thy thirst it is slaked, I wish thee farewell."

"Would that I parched in the desert sand,
Nor had ever been cool in this leafy land!

"And would that I bleached in the desert sere,
Nor had ever been blest from thy fountain clear!"

A NAY-WORD

In earnest if I love thee? Or ever I reply,
Forgive me, and remember how much in love doth
    lie,
      How much doth lie.

Love's duty and love's passion breathe not with
    mortal breath;
Pure love is joy and sorrow, sweet love is life and
    death,
      Is life and death.

Indeed, I do not love thee, I love thee not, ah, no;
Indeed, I cannot love thee, I care not for thee so,
    Alas! not so.

THE MENDED VIOL

It lieth in thine heart, I know,
    To play the movement o'er;
The instrument will not bestow
    The grace it gave before.

With pains let pardon be implored,
    Forgiveness thou shalt earn;
Note after note, and chord by chord,
    The music will return.

THE LAND OF THE LOST

At deep of night, in lonely bower, upon a muse I fell;
A gentle dream conveyed my soul where fallen spirits dwell.

They seemed so sad, they looked so fair, I gazed and marvelled long;
A single shape, a face I knew, came forward from the throng.

"Dear friend," she cried, "dear parted friend, 't is pleasure thee to greet;
Ere thy return, a kiss bestow, thy lips they are so sweet."

I kissed her lips, "Herein," she said, "I seal thee mine, dear heart;
For thou hast kissed, thy home is here, O never to depart."

BEGGARY

An alms for living
    I ask of thee;
Thou, after giving,
    Shalt wealthier be.

A coin of the largesse
    Thou wilt not retain,
A chord of the music
    Thou canst not restrain;

A smile of thy summer,
    If winter frown,
A leaf of thy laurel,
    If honor crown

A memory gentle,
    And once a year,
Over buried fancy
    A sigh, a tear:

BEGGARY

Such alms for living
    I ask of thee;
Thou, after giving,
    Shalt wealthier be.

FAIRIES' HILL

He hunted by field, he hunted by fell;
    When died away the sunset beam,
A cloud of sleep closed over his eyes,
    And his heart grew faint with a dream.

He lighted down at an oaken grove,
    By the rein his courser he bound;
His head was propped on a gnarlèd root,
    Apart from a grassy mound.

Came midnight, oped the fairy doors,
    The fairy halls were ashine;
A lady stepped forth from the Fairies' Hill,
    To serve the stranger with wine.

She bore in her hands a silver grail,
    As she passed to the hunter's place;
She stooped to his seat, and proffered the bowl;
    The twain gazed face to face.

"Sweet sister, is it truly thou?
    And, sister, farest thou well?
Is it joy to drink of the fairies' cup,
    And with the fairies dwell?"

The silver slipt between her hands,
    The liquor on moss was shed:
"More fortunate she at our mother's door
    Who seeketh the dole of bread,

"And happier one who shivering waits
    For the robe of a mercy cold,
Than it is to be fed of the fairies' feast,
    Arrayed in the silk and the gold!"

"My hunter hath a flying speed;
    Sweet sister, mount behind,
And I will bear thee so far away
    That the fairies shall never find,

"Will carry thee hence to a shelter safe,
    Where nevermore needest thou fear
To be charmed with the charm and spelled with the spell,
    And be ruled by the fairies here."

"And if thy steed were wingèd with thought,
    So far thou couldst never go,
But I must be back in the Fairies' Hill,
    Or ever the morn doth glow."

The cloud of sleep closed over his eyes,
    He fell to dreaming anew;
When next he awaked, the dawn was gray,
    And cold on his forehead the dew.

RED-ROSE-WOOD

When I was young, and a simple youth,
    A-wooing behooved me to ride;
I rode as far as the red-rose-wood,
    And it pleased me there to abide.

I lighted down at the red-rose-wood,
    I fell on a slumber deep;
Forth from her bower came the fairy queen
    To waken me out of sleep.

Forth from her bower came the fairy queen,
    In my ear low murmured she:
"Hark what I say, thou beautiful youth,
    To-night to dwell with me?

"To-night with me, thou beautiful youth,"
    She murmured low in mine ear,
"And my damsel shall sing thee a fairy song,
    If it pleaseth thee to hear."

The fairy was wise, she knew her lay,
    A spell of delight she began,
That the rushing river she bound to be still,
    The river that swiftly ran;

The rushing river she bound to be still,
    That poureth over the linn;
The trout that darts in the foamy pool,
    He stirred with never a fin;

The spotted deer, that leaps in the wood,
    Was fleet of foot no more;
The nightingale, that pines on the bough,
    Her melody was o'er.

The fairies were dancing out and in,
    They dancèd all in a band;
I gazed and gazed, poor simple youth,
    While I leaned my head on my hand.

THE LAST WORDS

(1214)

WILD waxed the mirth of the royal feast;
Before the king stood an aged priest.

"The Lady Ellen, from cloister," he said,
"Biddeth these maids to her dying bed."

Dark grew the brow of the castle's lord;
With an angry motion he spurned the board.

"Mount, mount, my daughters, mount and ride,
While starry-clear is the eventide."

They sped so fast, that when night was late,
The troop rode in at the convent gate.

They mounted up by a turret stair;
They entered a chamber, narrow and bare.

The naked walls and the foot-stones cold
Were shrouded with silk and with cloth of gold.

THE LAST WORDS

On a pallet low Lady Ellen lay;
Death stood at her feet, a shadow gray.

She opened her dimmèd eyes to see;
She signed to her side the princesses three.

"Christina, eldest born," she cried,
"How well becometh thee thy pride!

"This archèd brow, this tressèd hair,
One day shall Sweden's circle wear.

"Thy summer, Benedicta, be
A season merciful, like thee.

"But Katrine! O beloved, desired!
Thy youth with sweetness how attired!

"For thee I fear, or soon or late,
The image of thy mother's fate,

"The armèd hand, the forced embrace,
Then coldness, calumny, disgrace,

"And robbery of mother's right,
Her earnèd comfort and delight."

Exclaimed the king, "While yet we live,
If thee I harmed, that wrong forgive."

A scarlet flush to the pale cheek came,
The wasted eyes lit up with a flame:

"The guilt that on thy head doth lie,
That crime condone nor God nor I!"

She turned her face against the wall;
A terror fell on the courtiers all.

Dismayed, her daughters fled the cell;
From the tower pealed out her passing-bell.

THE SISTERS

"O SISTER, sister, hath my care, my rescue been in vain?
Day after day, before mine eyes, I watch thee droop and wane.
Have I not fed thee from my board, and robed thee from my store?
Have I not loved thee from my life? What could I give thee more?"

"To this wild heart, this altered fate, thou hast been kind, I know;
One final hope, one further boon, remaineth to bestow,
The pilgrim staff, the palmer's gown, to wander forth alone,
Where I may toil, where I may serve, unfollowed and unknown."

THE SISTERS

"Alas, what savage cruelty thy hardness hath designed!
Under what planet wert thou born to render thee unkind?
Myself to shine in cloth of gold, and thou to wear the frieze?
Thou tasked in foreign slavery, and I enthroned at ease!"

"There be for whom the diamonds shine, to whom the pearls are dear,
And others live whose bosoms proud the jewels brand and sere;
Let me go forth secure to dwell with souls as poor as I;
Sweet sister, thou shalt grant me peace, content no more deny."

FUNERAL MARCH

LET earth to earth be resignèd;
    Rest in peace.
Let soul with soul be enshrinèd;
    Rest in peace.
As thy deed, so thy memory lowly,
To love alone shall be holy;
March, march, in order and slowly,
    Rest in peace.

The comrades who battled about thee,
    Rest in peace.
What task shall be theirs without thee?
    Rest in peace.
Thy pride, adversity scorning,
Their beacon, their hope, and their warning,
Beheld the night like the morning,
    Rest in peace.

For fates severe wert thou singled;
    Rest in peace.
World's woe for thee hath been mingled;
    Rest in peace.
Thy crown, of sorrow's designing,
Showed thorns and roses entwining,
No laurel, no myrtle combining,
    Rest in peace.

Alas, that so hath befallen!
    Rest in peace.
Thy flower ungathered hath fallen;
    Rest in peace.
No maid, in thee for her lover,
Shall deep under deep discover,
Clear height over height above her,
    Rest in peace.

With hero's heart hast thou striven;
    Rest in peace.
A soldier's life hast thou given;
    Rest in peace.
We make no lamenting o'er thee;
Forgive the sigh, we implore thee;
Thy right of calm we restore thee,
    Rest in peace.

THE LONELY OCEAN

A BLUE and lonely ocean
    Encompasseth an isle ;
With many-voicèd motion
    It soundeth all the while.

A merry infant playeth
    With never-wearied joy;
Beside a pool delayeth
    To launch his floating toy.

Time cometh, when he pleases
    To dare the shining sea ;
He flieth before breezes,
    White sail, and billows free.

'Twixt hope and terror only
    He tosseth by and by,
A waif on ocean lonely,
    Beholding sea and sky.

THE FOUNT OF TEARS

THEE like a babe all innocently born,
    Sweet fount, would I behold, and joy to view
Above thy quiet pool a rival morn
    Repose in silent change of clouds and blue;
    Of slender rushes on thy verge that grew,
Forget-me-nots, and one pale rose forlorn,
    My coronet would weave, to sing the while,
    And, wistful, woo Love's tear, as if indeed Love's smile.

Within thy neighboring woodland would I make
    My pensive quest, its sacred sprites to meet, —
Youth, musing-pale, with Honor, hot to take
    His rapid prey ere rival Death defeat;
    Free-wandering Fancies in thy wild would greet,
Fair Hope like Sorrow masked; and haply wake
    A forest-slumbering Thought, that in surprise
    On me would lift the lids of childish frightened eyes.

THE FOUNT OF TEARS

Even to-day to thee have I recourse,
    Albeit years have cruel wisdom bred,
And taught me how thy plenty, dangerous source!
    From that perpetual-changing deep is fed,
    Wherewith our fates are singly islanded;
The seal may be unclosèd, and with force
    The child who by thy current doth remain,
    One free and mounting billow render to the main,

Yet for mine own part may it never be,
    As others are constrained, that I forbear
To rove thy haunted glades, or fill from thee
    The mingled cup of gratitude and care;
    No more by fondness armed, must these despair
To reckon with heart-aiming Memory,
    And, foreign to affection and to pain,
    Thank every dawning day for sunshine or for rain.

But he who keeps a remnant of Love's shield,
    Albeit Time-piercèd, doth not find it so;
To him thy welcome fount a draught doth yield
    Chill with refreshing more than cold with woe;
    Beside thy marge celestial flowers grow,
And blooms of comfort in thy nooks concealed;
    So holy seems thy well, that to give o'er
    The pilgrimage, would be to live and breathe
        no more.

THE WELL OF THE WORLD'S END

"What water to this twilight dell
    Doth lonely glimmer lend?"
"Fair wanderer, 't is called the Well
    Of the World's End."

"Pray, is it sweet, the rivulet
    That icily doth flow?"
"Its virtue maketh to forget
    Desire and woe."

"What duty thine, who lingerest late,
    Pale feature veilèd o'er?"
"Dear child of earth, I am thy Fate;
    Inquire no more."

A BIRTHDAY

A THRUSH upon a maple bough gave all his mind
    and sang;
The hill was green, the maple bare, the road and
    valley rang.
I listened to the song afar, I heard the tune anear;
The burden went: "Fair Earth to-day is younger by
    a year,
  Fair Earth to-day, fair Earth to-day, is younger
    by a year."

Or if I came, or if I went, the voice would not be
    mute;
It chanted on in sweeter change than viol, harp, or
    lute.
I learned the melody by heart, it chimeth in mine
    ear;
The burden went: "Fair Earth to-day is younger by
    a year,
  Fair Earth to-day, fair Earth to-day, is younger
    by a year."

MAY MORNING

PURPLE and pink is the twilight of May,
    Fresh of a morning early;
Awaken the birds with the waking of day,
    And I love my love so dearly.

Apple-blossoms are blithe to see,
    Fresh of a morning early;
Green are the leaves of the maple-tree,
    And I love my love so dearly.

An oriole builds on a hanging bough,
    Fresh of a morning early;
Hark, to his mate he calleth now,
    And I love my love so dearly.

THE SCARLET TANAGER

A FLAME, a wandering fire,
With wavering desire
   From bough to bough,
Thou wingèd, wondrous thing!
Of glad, of golden spring
   The soul art thou,
      A flame, a wandering fire.

Thy strange, thy scarlet gleam,
Will glisten through my dream
   The livelong year;
O pure, O holy May!
O blithe, O blessed way
   I travel here!
      A flame, a wandering fire.

ORPHEUS TO APOLLO

[ON THE PICTURE BY COROT]

Lo, falleth o'er yon Eastern height
    A beam of crimson fire!
To thee, pure fount of song and light,
    I lift the golden lyre!

Shine thou upon the instrument,
    Smite every thrilling chord!
Make every tone obedient
    As arrow of its lord!

From skies by thee illumed to-day
    And lands thou shalt behold,
Confer a glory, that the lay
    Rise full and clear and bold!

And when thine happiness shall leave
    The West with roses crowned,
As grateful let the hymn of eve
    In peace and honor sound.

THE LAKE AND THE RIVER

THE RIVER

Thou gazest into heaven
    With eyes so blue and glad;
In white and fragrant lilies
    Is thy Undinè clad.

THE LAKE

Thou fallest from the mountain,
    Thou flowest by the hill;
A thousand singing streamlets
    Thy rushing currents fill.

THE RIVER

The roses of the sunset
    Upon thy breast remain,
So pure the heart thou yieldest,
    So free of selfish stain.

THE LAKE AND THE RIVER

THE LAKE

Thy broad and gleaming splendor
    Hath nought to envy mine,
When on thy swollen water
    The solemn glories shine.

VIOLET

Thou bloomest so secret,
    So modest, so dear;
A perfume, a comfort,
    Revealeth thee near.

Who cherished may keep thee,
    With safety enclose,
Need seek not, need sigh not,
    For lily and rose.

WATER-LILIES

I CARRY white water-lilies, white lilies of starry grace;
I lay them beside thy bosom, I twine them about thy face.

Thou liest serene and stately, adorned with thy beauty the while;
Out of a tender silence on me thou seemest to smile.

I leave the light of mine eyes, I leave the hope of mine heart;
Beloved, bestow thy peace, thy peace with me to depart.

MOONLIGHT

THE breathing of ocean
    Is peaceful to-night;
The golden moon claspeth
    His bosom with light.

Her glory in heaven
    Doth reign and prevail;
Its torches she quencheth
    In mystery pale;

The chamber she floodeth
    Where calm thou dost lie;
Thy dream be illumined
    As water and sky!

THE LIGHTHOUSE

A MILD and wakeful beacon
    Glows lonely o'er the deep;
Above its crowning lantern
    Do scornful waters leap.

Now boiling surges eddy,
    Now welling billows pour;
Resounding breakers thunder
    Along a granite shore.

Homebound, a white sail neareth
    The pure and friendly light;
A moment more, it veereth,
    Concealed by foam and night.

THE STORM

His brow was dark, his glance was stern, the storm-
    king in the north;
With ire he bade his helpers rise, he sent his heralds
    forth;
He made proclaim his holy war through all his
    realm so wide;
'T was cried aloud upon the height, and in the deep
    't was cried.

Behold, his hosts are mustering, by hill and glen
    they come,
Each lonely path is echoing as if with fife and
    drum;
I see the glinting of their arms on highland and on
    plain;
Myself have taken sword and spear to foray in their
    train.

THE STORM

Blow, clarions, blow! Ye cannot peal so bold as my desire!
Wave, banners, wave! Ye cannot flame so clear as my heart's fire!
Shout, warriors, shout! Of thousand tones a single voice be made,
Hurrah, hurrah, our master's war, hurrah for his crusade!

THE FOREST

Great harp of the mighty forest, thy many voices
  prepare
To sound in a single music, be born in this golden air;
Deep joy hath he in the forest who liveth and reigneth
  alone;
The spirit of every creature doth breathe and blend
  in his own.

O rocks so ancient and stainèd, O trees that rustle
  and shine,
Green oaks that mantle the highlands, and sunlighted
  stems of the pine,
Pure waters that murmur and glisten in silence from
  mosses fed,
Bright world of marvels and glimpses, and blue-
  gleaming sky overhead,

THE FOREST

Dark curve of the Eastern ocean, glad peaks of the boundless West,
From morn to even unclouded, apparelled in sapphire blest,
Mine heart is free and rejoiceth, hath learned the rhymes that belong;
Wild harp of the lonely forest, prelude the chords of the song.

AN OUTLOOK

THE glances, the spaces
    Of innocent day;
The welcomes, the graces
    Of flower-breathing May;

The city extending
    So mistily fair,
A human heart blending
    With sunshine and air;

Near oak-forests showing
    Now red, now pale;
Pink apple-trees blowing,
    The spires of the vale;

Far peace-loving mountains
    That cloudlessly gleam;
Pure lakes and sweet fountains
    That harborward stream;

AN OUTLOOK

Round ocean yonder;
    Blue heaven o'er, —
Mine, mine, O wonder!
    Forevermore!

THOUGHT-BIRTHS

Star-risings, and the march of orbs that shone,
A master scanned, and studied paths unknown,
Till out of darkness, seed of thought was sown.

For birthpang's sake, for midnights of despair,
Since worth from toil derives, and love from care,
He prized his Thought, and called it right and fair.

Companions dwelt the twain; and overwise,
As one by knowledge cheated of surprise,
His offspring measured life with strange sad eyes.

But wingèd Thoughts it doth not well become
In infant nest to linger; these must roam,
Thus saith the law, in quest of other home.

So winged the wanderer forth, and, self-afraid,
A shelter long required, until he made
His second birth in spirit of a maid.

Of simple house, of gentle nature, she
In quiet had been nurtured, pure and free
As in her sight, the emerald-changing sea.

For her desire did floating lilies shine
To rim the azure lake in silver line,
Pink roses tangle, and the wild grape twine.

Upon such terms she stood with Day and Night,
That little pleasures, deemed our human right,
Her face would color with a swift delight.

In this new world the Thought remained, as one
Who joy of youthful friendship hath begun,
And, pleased, discovers he himself is young.

Now came the master's hour to make appear
Before the world, his gain; she found it dear,
Among the rest, to listen and revere.

Deep-voiced, and burdened with life's freight of woe,
He charted secular tides that ebb and flow,
Proved wane of stars that erst did regnant glow,

Calm guides divine; then suddenly befell
As when a gazer in an elfin well
In its clear deep beholds the fairy dwell;

For in the glances lifted to his own
He met his Thought, his creature, his alone,
But oh, how altered from expression known!

A look, as if wide Wisdom's house were meant
A roof for peace, a frame for ornament
Of rainbow-woven joy and world's content.

The speaker ceased, and, homeward-turning, fled
Pursuit of thanks and praises; with bowed head,
"From mouth of babes," low to himself he said.

ANY HARPER TO HIS HARP

My passion and thy pleasure,
    My harp, will not unite;
I honor golden morning,
    Thou hymnest starry night.

Thy silence I awakened
    With chords that mournful rang;
The melody to heaven
    Arose, and soared, and sang.

Thy full and flowing river
    For rill of mine atones;
Like sun on falling water
    Are thy rainbow overtones.

The spirits of thy lovers
    With thee forever dwell,
One hath his royal palace,
    And one his hermit's cell;

ANY HARPER TO HIS HARP

One singeth consolation
    Of fruitful happy years;
One sigheth supplication
    Of lonely martyr-tears.

Delight, desire, and rapture,
    Despair, remorse, and fear,
Are born a single music,
    Harmonious and clear.

Mine harp, mine harp beloved!
    Fate hath to me been kind;
Some breathing of the summer,
    Some sweetness mayest thou find,

And with thine other voices
    In peace the essence blend,
Of one who was thy master,
    Thy minstrel, and thy friend!

TO THE SOUL

When over deep and silent summer night
    Mild planets shone,
Thou, thoughtful, gavest to those pilgrims bright
    Looks like their own.

When wreathèd hours embraced, in kissing maze,
    A careless band,
Thou, nunlike mid the revel, mute, didst raise
    A warning hand.

When on the lonely vigil, pale, increased
    One streak of morn,
Thou, wakeful, hast beheld the cruel East,
    And didst not mourn.

When, sorrow-bold, I made my prayer to Woe:
    "Be heaven of mine!"
The answering goddess freed her veil, and lo!
    The eyes were thine!

DECORATION

In gleaming chestnut glade,
Where early June hath made
The freshest, blithest shade,
    Level and low,
They lie apart, alone,
Never a lettered stone;
One — but the grave unknown —
    In life a foe.

Desire no worshipped name;
The partial cry of Fame
Meteth nor praise nor blame,
    No titles here;
From mill, from shop, and plough,
These came, no record how,
To one promotion now,
    Common and clear.

DECORATION

For them the stern advance,
The field, the ambulance,
The pang, the mortal trance,
    The stranger's earth;
Sweet youth must we resign
To wither and decline,
Why alter Nature's sign
    Of hope and mirth?

Is it reply to say,
Joy dwells with Spring alway,
Winter's forgot in May,
    Sorrow in flowers?
At last, at last, though late,
Have veered the winds of hate;
The sowing was their fate,
    The harvest, — ours.

Blooms of the forest wild,
Full many a little child,
As innocently mild,
    Shall reverent throw;
To cover up their rest,
Our gardens yield their best,
The rarest, costliest,
    Yet fairer, — no.

DECORATION

However cities proud
Thunder with cannon loud,
Or wave a gaudy cloud
    Of flags on high,
That people liveth poor
Untrained by memories pure,
To suffer, to endure, —
    At need, to die.

NEW ROCHELLE, N. Y., 1878.

GREETING

Beside the tides of Atlantic, that flow so clear and so cold,
By feet of the shining Sierras, by western Gate of Gold,
Where the billowy seas of the prairie roll green under skies of light,
In glens of the leafy highlands, on fields where the cotton is white;

I hail thee, I greet thee, my brother! Receive the heart and the hand,
In the name of the bountiful parent, the dearly-beloved land!
She weareth the mantle of plenty, she reigneth from sea to sea;
As wide as the realm of the mother the thoughts of the children be.

1893.

THE TEMPLE

My temple bright
I made on a height,
    Wide earth below;
Of marbles strange
Did columns change
    In many a row.

Each glorious wall
Was storied with all
    That gods befell;
In outer court,
For world's resort,
    A healing well.

Pure holy days
With robes and praise
    Did clergy keep;
Alone divine,
One grave, one shrine,
    To kneel and weep.

REQUIEM

FROM northern earth, how bloomed this stranger blest?
Beloved and cherished upon Nature's breast.

Shall dear companions sigh above his grave? —
While forests murmur, and while grasses wave.

Who harboreth his thoughts, now he is gone? —
No second friend; they trusted him alone.

Where gain of life, since he hath found repose? —
Maybe a bluer sky, a redder rose.

1875.

EROICA

Where plant the lily of my heart, my gentle lily, where?
O generous should be the earth, and innocent the air.

A grave above the river blue, a soldier's grave I know;
There, gazing o'er the paths he trod, shall my pure lily grow.

Its root pierce deep in sacred soil, to thrive for many years;
It shall be nourished by my hopes, and watered with my tears.

When falls the hour, in perfect grace will bloom my lily white,
A splendor in the sunny morn, a fragrance in the night.

"O Earth, how free thy bounties are! O Sun, what
    warmth is thine!
O Life, how glorious thy boon! O Nature, how
    divine!

"The greenwood here, in budding May, how blithe-
    some to behold!
How worthy its October robe of crimson and of gold!

"Rejoicing birds, in golden prime, what concert do
    they keep!
The harmonies of autumn gales, their chords how
    grand and deep!

"The stream, the town, the clasping hills, the city
    domed and dim,
A million joys, a million woes, combining in a hymn!

"For me the essence of the whole, the anthem's soul
    of truth,
One passion chaste, one holy flame, one sacrifice of
    youth!"

So shall I cry, and here resort at morning and at
 eve;
Care-laden will my feet approach, calm-hearted shall
 I leave.

When day hath deepened into dusk, and due mine
 earnèd rest,
This lily shall bestow a flower to lay upon my breast.

PEACE

When morning beameth on the plain, and thy forsaken home,
Then peaceful in the eastern ray shine river, spires, and dome;
And when the summer twilights pale, and rose and purple die,
The air of even breathes so low, that scarce is heard the sigh.

When earth remembereth to be green, and mirthful robins sing,
Along the quiet lonely path a pilgrim fareth Spring,
A moment museth o'er her child, as youthful and as fair,
Then gently passeth on her way, to leave a violet there.

A MEMORY

A LAMP I know of a merciful ray;
It burneth forever, by night and by day.

It maketh a safe and a pleasant room;
It shineth far, if deep be the gloom.

The darkness I welcome for love of its grace;
My lamp hath the light of a holy face.

THE END

The titlepage of this book has been designed by Adelene Moffat, after an Italo-Greek vase in possession of the author.

www.ingramcontent.com/pod-product-compliance
Lightning Source LLC
Chambersburg PA
CBHW020227090426
42735CB00010B/1616